BOOK 4

Celebrated Lyrical Solos

7 Solos in Romantic Styles for Intermediate Pianists

Robert D. Vandall

Students all love to play fast and showy pieces, but there is another side to performing that needs to be developed: the lyrical side. Beautiful melodies need to be shaped musically and balanced properly against the accompaniment. The ability to bend the tempo and play with flexibility also results in expressive playing. Colorful harmonies and their movement can create a sound world that can be molded into beautiful moments as well.

The pieces in *Celebrated Lyrical Solos, Book 4* are designed to aid students with musicality when playing lyrical music. I have endeavored to include pieces with a variety of tempos and moods. While every piece may not necessarily focus on lyrical styles throughout, each has a section that will help students develop skills in lyrical playing. Look for the many ways that the pieces in these books can be balanced and molded into something beautiful. Feel, listen and enjoy the many lyrical moods of these solos.

Robert D. Vandall

Contents

ISBN-10: 0-7390-5077-X
ISBN-13: 978-0-7390-5077-4

Alfred

Lullaby

Robert D. Vandall

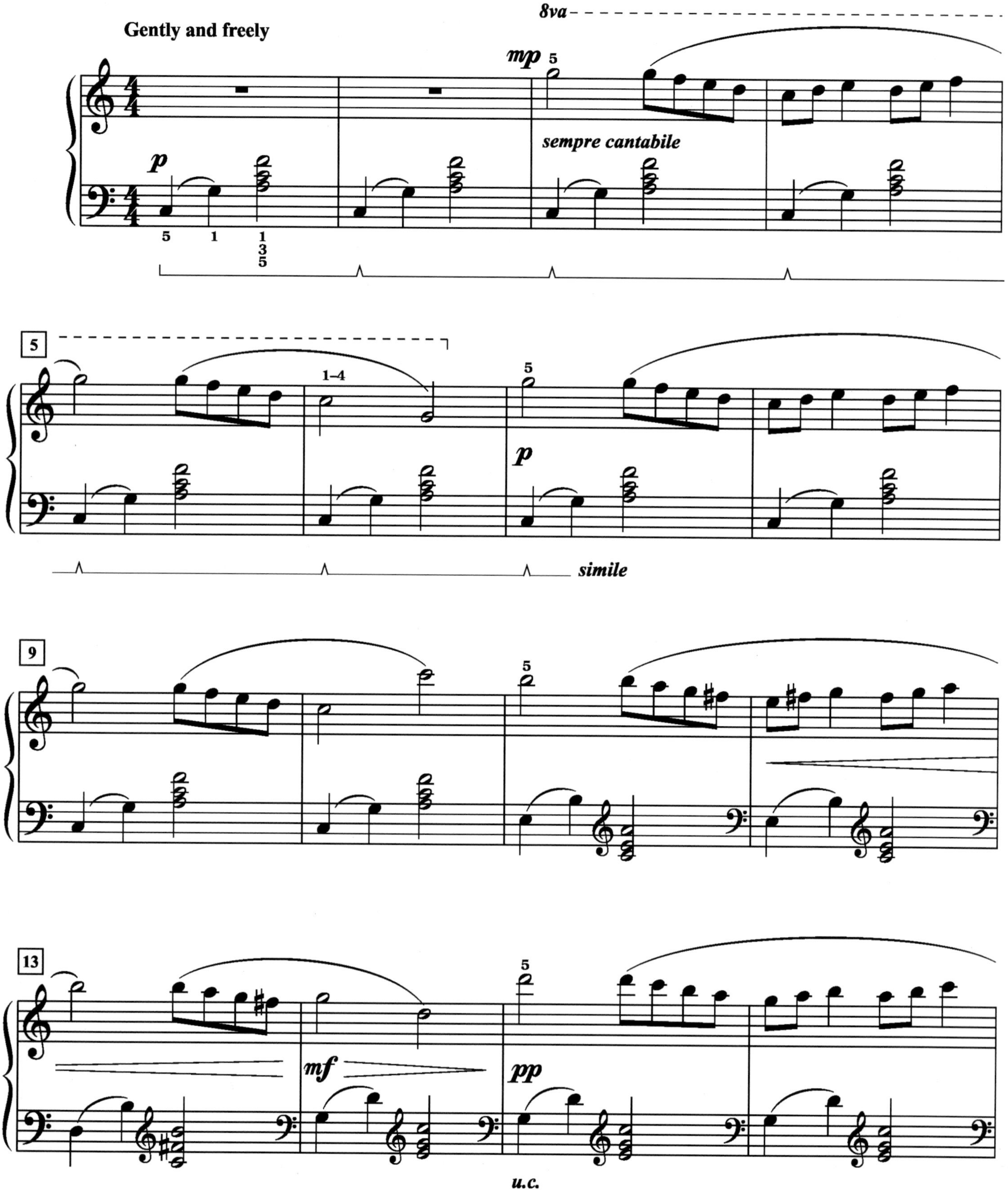

a tempo
8va
17
poco rit.
5
mp
t.c.
21
1–4
5
p
25
5
29
mf
5
pp
u.c.

33
a tempo
8va
poco rit.
mp
t.c.
37
1–4
p
40
43
8va
mp
rit.
p
1–5
8va

Enchanted Carillon

Robert D. Vandall

17
mp
p
22
mf
cresc.
27
f
mf
31
mp
p
pp ritenuto

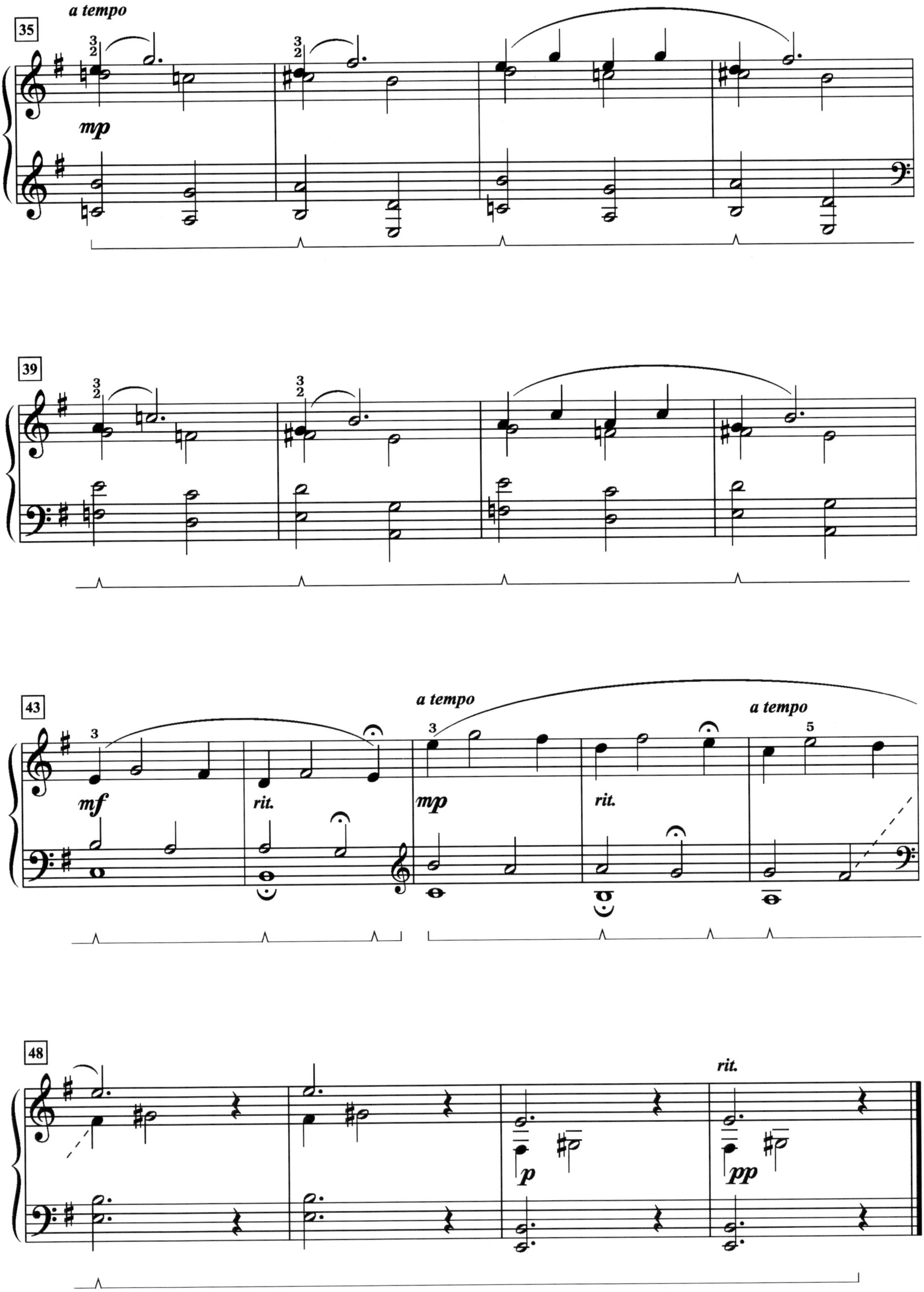
a tempo
35
mp
39
43
mf
rit.
a tempo
mp
rit.
a tempo
48
rit.
p
pp

Romance

Robert D. Vandall

Freely and expressively (♩ = ca. 144)

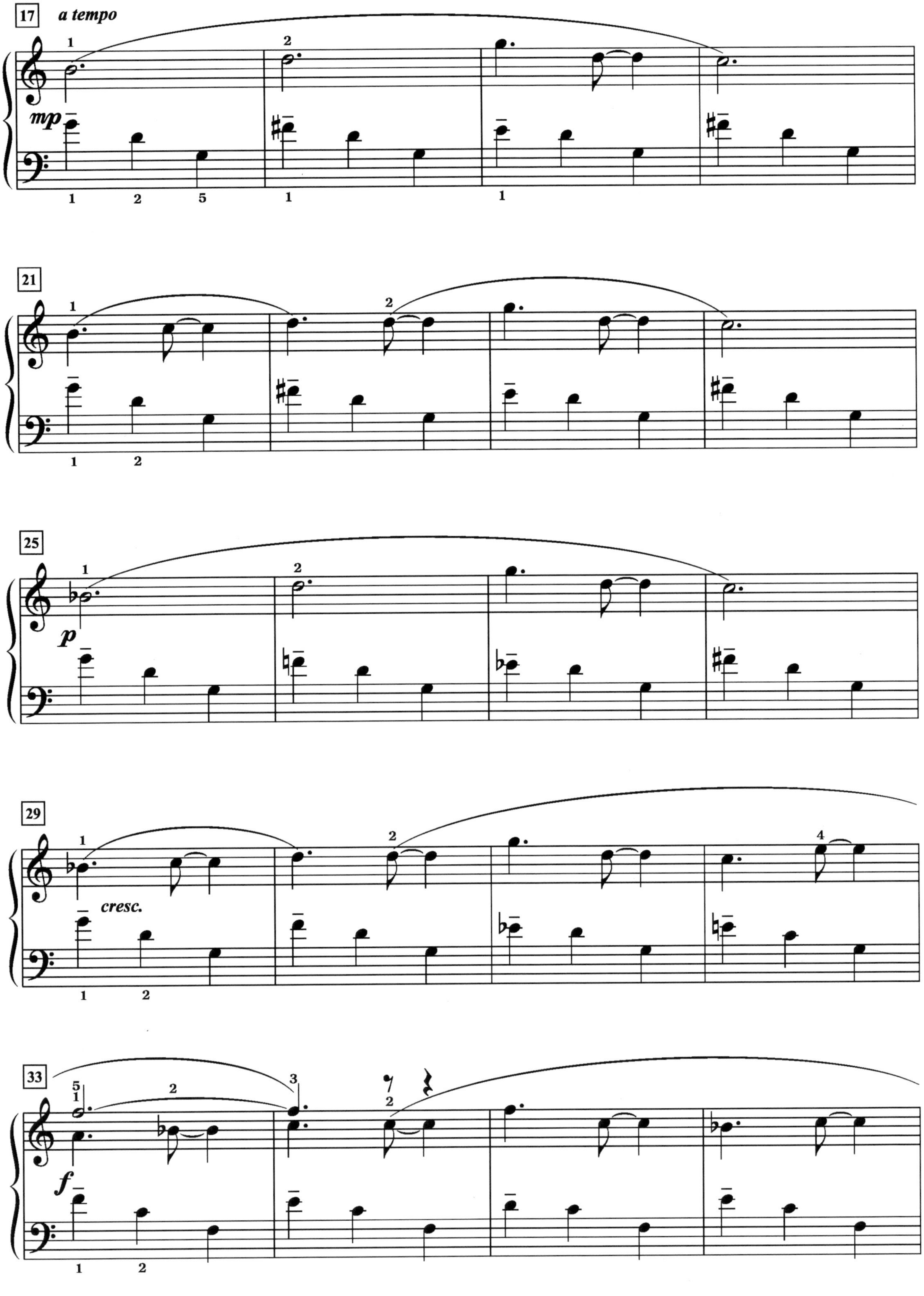
17
a tempo
mp
21
25
p
29
cresc.
33
f

37
rit. e dim.
41
a tempo
mp
simile
45
49
mf
mp

53
cresc.
57
f
61
dim.
65
mp
p
rit.
LH
LH

Forever Friends

Robert D. Vandall

Andantino espressivo e molto rubato (♩ = ca. 96)

22
a tempo
cresc.
f
rit.
mp
27
mf
31
mp
cresc.
35
longa
meno mosso
a tempo
ff
rit.
mp
39
mf
f
dim.
rit.
p

End of Summer

Robert D. Vandall

Allegretto con rubato

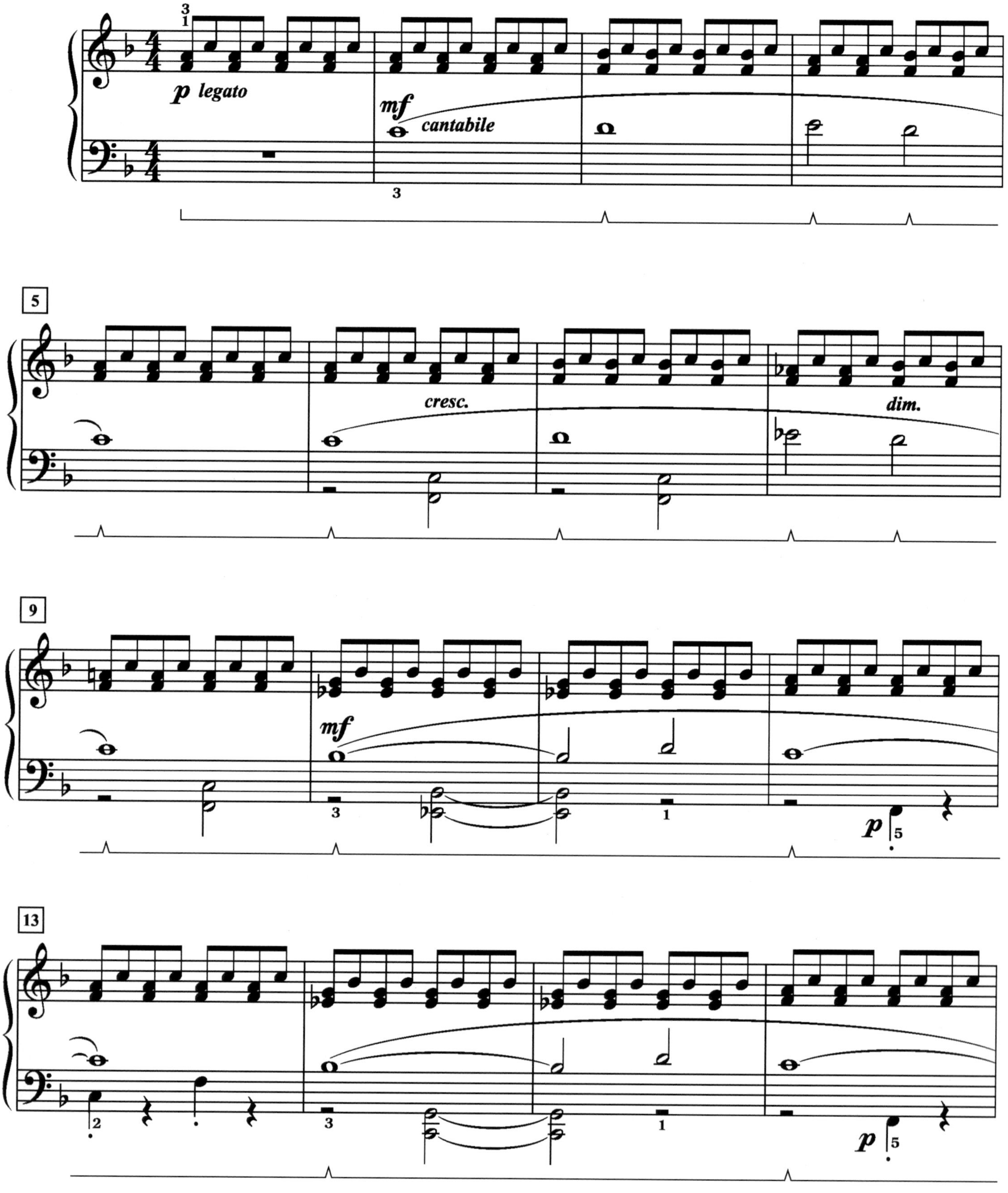

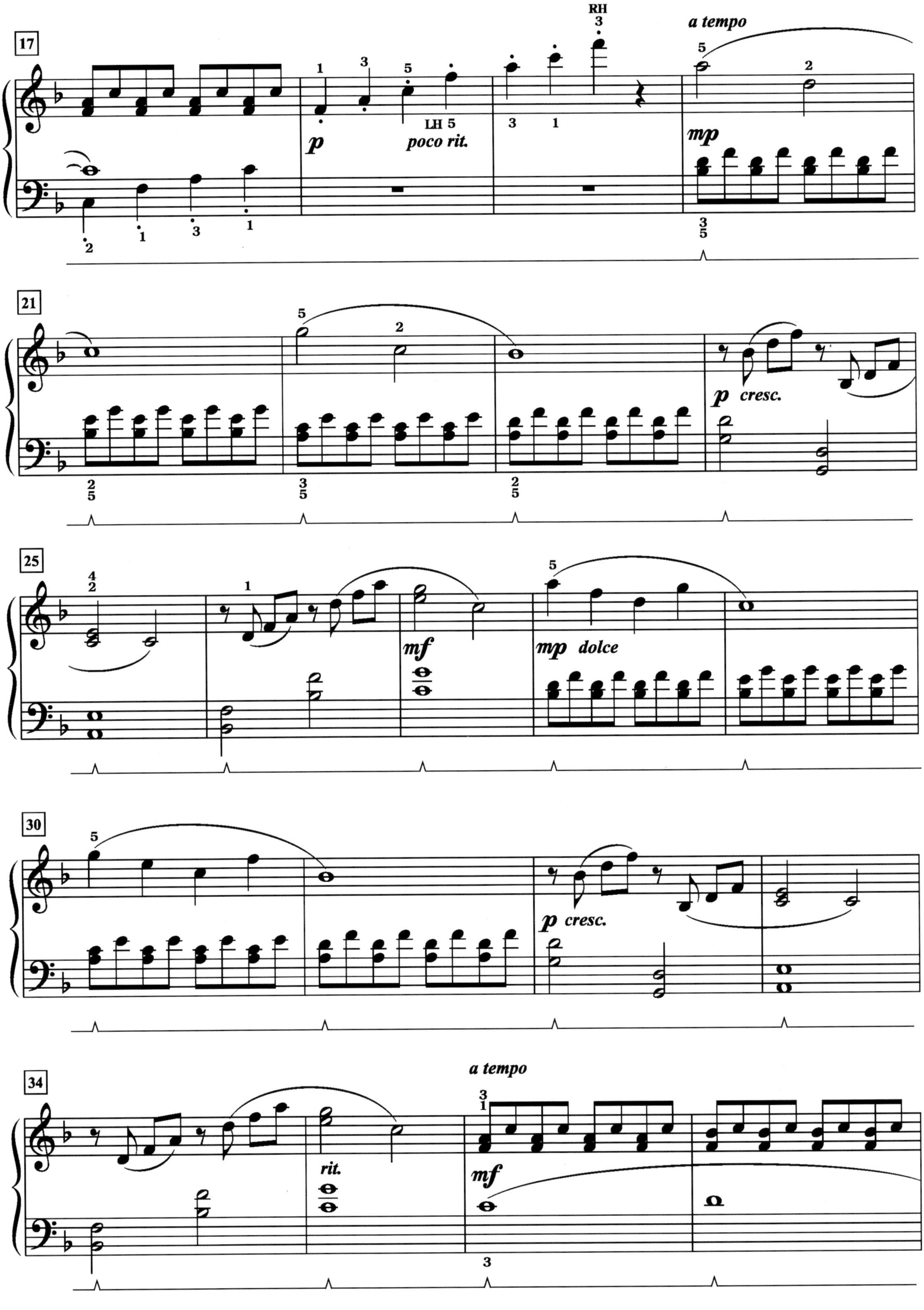
17
RH
a tempo
LH
poco rit.
p
mp
21
p cresc.
25
mf
mp dolce
30
p cresc.
34
a tempo
rit.
mf

38
cresc.
42
dim.
mf
46
f
dim. e rit.
p
50
a tempo
mf
p
rit.
LH 5
RH

Painter's Palette

Robert D. Vandall

Allegretto con rubato (♩ = ca. 88)

17
f
pp
f
pp
21
p cresc.
f
25
pp
p cresc.
29
f
pp
f
pp rit.

33
a tempo
mf
mp
36
cresc.
40
f
pp
43
f
pp
mp
p
rit.

Crystal Falls

Robert D. Vandall

9
mf
p
11
cresc.
dim. e poco rit.
13
a tempo
p
15
rit.
17
a tempo
pp
RH
u.c.

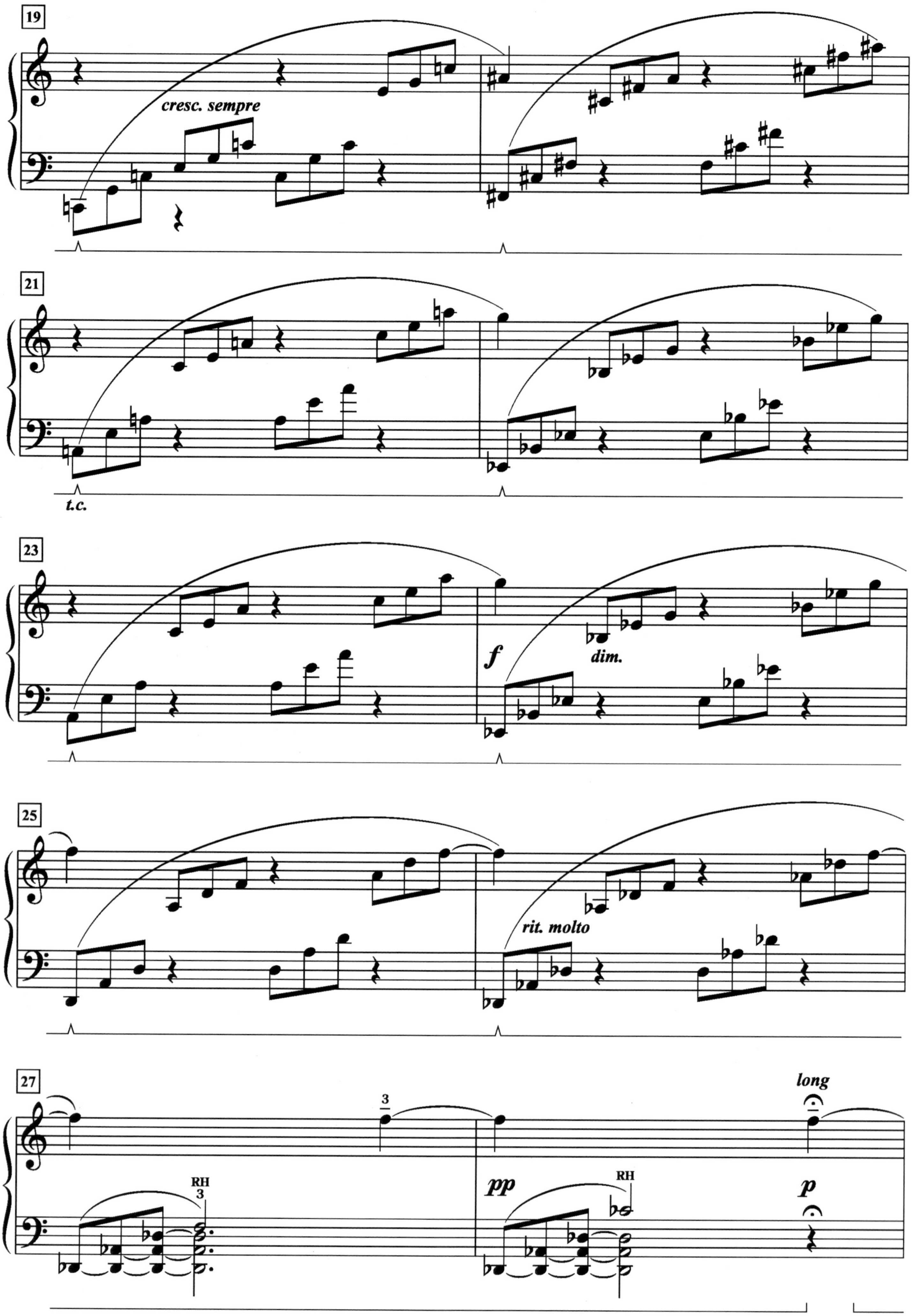
19
cresc. sempre
21
t.c.
23
f
dim.
25
rit. molto
27
3
RH
3
pp
RH
long
p

29
a tempo
LH over
31
33
35
cresc.
37
mf
p

39
cresc.
dim. e poco rit.
3
41
a tempo
p
43
pp
u.c.
45
rit.